Healing in Every Book of the Bible
by Dr. Lester Sumrall

Sumrall Publishing
P.O. Box 12
South Bend, IN

Copyright © 2002

Healing in Every Book of the Bible

ISBN 0-937580-29-5

New Expanded Edition

Published by Sumrall Publishing
P.O. Box 12
South Bend, Indiana 46624
www.sumrallpublishing.com

All rights reserved. Contents and/or cover may not be reproduced without written permission of the publisher.

Printed in the United States of America.

All Scripture quotations are from the *King James Version of the Holy Bible*.

All revisions/additions made to the 2002 Edition of "Healing in Every Book of the Bible" were taken directly from Dr. Lester Sumrall's "Legacy of Faith Study Bible." Published by Thomas Nelson Publishers, 1997.

Table of Contents

Introduction

Hebrews 4:12-13, *For the word of God is quick, and powerful, and sharper than any two-edged sword, piercing even to the dividing asunder of soul and spirit, and of the joints and marrow, and is a discerner of the thoughts and intents of the heart.*

v. 13, *Neither is there any creature that is not manifest in his sight: but all things are naked and opened unto the eyes of him with whom we have to do.*

When you allow the Word of God to burn in you, everything that is of Him remains, and all that is of yourself is destroyed. Maybe that is why some people don't like to intimately seek God. Maybe that is why some don't like to get involved with the Word—studying, reading, and praying. If you get too close to the fire of God, those false foundations will get burned; but the same fire that burns and destroys false foundations, burns and purifies the spiritual truths within you.

It is only through the Word that the consuming fire is exposed to our lives to produce healing. This world is hurting, suffering, and dying because it needs the Word, manifesting, purging, healing, and setting free. God is willing to heal every aspect of your life: your marriage, your finances, your emotions, your relationships, your attitude, and your body.

Are you willing to allow the Word of God to get close enough to you to work its changing power through you? I encourage you to read and be lifted in your faith, and then reach out to the Lord with expectation!

—Stephen Sumrall
Senior Pastor,
Christian Center Church

Foreword

Dr. Lester Sumrall
1913-1996

The voice of Dr. Lester Sumrall remains prominent in the Christian world today. More than 65 years of ministry in over 100 nations made Dr. Sumrall a respected source of wisdom and understanding. He was an author, teacher, missionary, evangelist, and the pastor and founder of Christian Center Church in South Bend, Indiana. Throughout his lifetime, Dr. Sumrall worked tirelessly to fulfill The Great Commission by carrying the gospel to the ends of the earth. In 1957 he founded LeSEA, a multi-faceted global outreach. Today LeSEA's outreaches blanket the world through television, satellite, FM and shortwave radio, and LeSEA Global Feed the Hungry®. Would you like to be a part of feeding the spirit, soul, and body of the hungry? Call today! **1-888-TEAM-FTH**
1-888-8326-384

24-Hour Prayerline
(574) 291-1010

www.lesea.com

-1-

The Origin of Sickness and Disease

There was no sin, sickness, disease, or any evil work in the Garden of Eden until Adam and Eve rebelled against God by eating of the fruit of the tree God had commanded they not partake of. They voluntarily broke covenant with God, which changed both their intimate relationship with God and their "perfectness" in spirit, soul, and body (Genesis 1:26-27; Genesis 2:17; Romans 5:12; Romans 6:23; Genesis 3:1-19).

God's command to Adam and Eve, as a part of His covenant with them, was:

Genesis 2:16-17, *And the LORD God commanded the man, saying, Of every tree of the garden thou mayest freely eat*:
v. 17, *But of the tree of the knowledge of good and evil, thou shalt not eat of it: for in the day that thou eatest thereof thou shalt surely die.*

Both Adam and Eve ate the fruit of the tree of the knowledge of good and evil. They received firsthand knowledge of all that is good and all that is evil. Because of their sin and rebellion against God, sin, sickness, and disease, and physical death entered the earth. Up to this time there was no sickness, plague, disease, or death.

In Genesis 3:16-19, God clearly states the result of Adam and Eve's disobedience:

Genesis 3:16-19, *Unto the woman he said, I will greatly multiply thy sorrow and thy conception; in sorrow thou shalt bring forth children; and thy desire shall be to thy husband, and he shall rule over thee.*

v. 17, *And unto Adam he said, Because thou hast hearkened unto the voice of thy wife, and hast eaten of the tree, of which I commanded thee, saying, Thou shalt not eat of it: cursed is the ground for thy sake; in sorrow shalt thou eat of it all the days of thy life;*

v. 18, *Thorns also and thistles shall it bring forth to thee; and thou shalt eat the herb of the field;*

v.19, *In the sweat of thy face shalt thou eat bread, till thou return unto the ground; for out of it wast thou taken: for dust thou art, and unto dust shalt thou return.*

SIN AND SICKNESS ARE RELATED

If all the men living were doctors, if all the women living on the face of the earth were nurses, and if all the homes on this earth were hospitals, the world would still be sick because sickness is highly related to sin, and sickness is a spiritual phenomenon in most cases.

In both the Old and New Testaments, sickness, disease, and plagues came as a result of sin against God. We see this same association of sin and sickness in John 5:14 and Mark 2:9:

John 5:14, *Afterward Jesus findeth him in the temple, and said unto him, Behold, thou art made whole: sin no more, lest a worse thing come unto thee.*

Mark 2:9, *Whether is it easier to say to the sick of the palsy, Thy sins be forgiven thee; or to say, Arise, and take up thy bed, and walk?*

A person whose spirit is healthy will rarely be sick in his body. An unhealthy spirit exists when a person is not in right relationship with God. A person whose spirit is low (beaten down with sin, discouragement, or depression) can pick up diseases like nobody's business.

To be sick in your spirit is the most dangerous of all illnesses. Sickness in your spirit can also be related and carried into your soulical and physical parts. A person who is sick in his spirit can very easily become sick in his emotions, sick in his mind, and for sure sick in his will to the point that he has no willpower to stand up and be the person God created him to be. That's the reason we have to keep the human spirit so strong. I don't believe that a person who is sick in his spirit can have a well body. It would be fatigued. But the good news is God can pick you up and heal your spirit!

SATAN IS THE AUTHOR AND PROPAGATOR OF SICKNESS

In Acts 10:38, Jesus identified Satan as the oppressor. *How God anointed Jesus of Nazareth with the Holy Ghost and with power: who went about doing good, and healing all that were oppressed of the devil; for God was with him.* Notice, Jesus healed all who were oppressed by the devil.

I have discovered that if God said it, He meant it. If He said it, it is true. If He said it, it works. All you've got to do is have faith in His promises.

Some Christians think that sickness is a blessing. They say, "Oh God made me sick so He can help me." For this to be true, God would have to contradict His Word in Acts 10:38. Satan is the oppressor — the author and propagator of sickness and disease and everything that is unlike God.

In Luke 13:11-16, Jesus openly acknowledged that Satan is the one who bound the woman with a spirit of infirmity for eighteen years:

Luke 13:11-16, *And, behold, there was a woman which had a spirit of infirmity eighteen years, and was bowed together, and could in no wise lift up herself.*

v. 12, *And when Jesus saw her, he called her to him, and said unto her, Woman, thou art loosed from thine infirmity.*

v. 13, *And he laid his hands on her: and immediately she was made straight, and glorified God.*

v. 14, *And the ruler of the synagogue answered with indignation, because that Jesus had healed on the sabbath day, and said unto the people, There are six days in which men ought to work: in them therefore come and be healed, and not on the sabbath day.*

v. 15, *The Lord then answered him, and said, Thou hypocrite, doth not each one of you on the sabbath loose his ox or his ass from the stall, and lead him away to watering?*

v. 16, *And ought not this woman, being a daughter of Abraham, whom Satan hath bound, lo, these eighteen years, be loosed from this bond on the sabbath day?*

In Mark 9:25, we again see a relationship between Satan's works (a deaf and dumb spirit) and the wholeness of a young boy. When Jesus cast the spirit out, the boy was set free. *When*

Jesus saw that the people came running together, he rebuked the foul spirit, saying unto him, Thou dumb and deaf spirit, I charge thee, come out of him, and enter no more into him.

In Mark 1:26, Jesus cast an unclean spirit out of a man, and he was made whole. *And when the unclean spirit had torn him, and cried with a loud voice, he came out of him.*

HEAVEN GIVES DIVINE HEALTH

I believe in the mighty healing process that comes down from Heaven, because God loves us, Jesus Christ loves us, and the Holy Spirit loves us. By the blood of Jesus we can receive total healing for the whole man — spirit, soul, and body.

Jesus was anointed to remove Satan's works. This truth is found in Luke 4:17-21:

Luke 4:17-21, *And there was delivered unto him the book of the prophet Esaias. And when he had opened the book, he found the place where it was written,*

v. 18, *The Spirit of the Lord is upon me, because he hath anointed me to preach the gospel to the poor; he hath sent me to heal the brokenhearted, to preach deliverance to the captives, and recovering of sight to the blind, to set at liberty them that are bruised,*

v. 19, *To preach the acceptable year of the Lord.*

v. 20, *And he closed the book, and he gave it again to the minister, and sat down. And the eyes of all them that were in the synagogue were fastened on him.*

v. 21, *And he began to say unto them, This day is this scripture fulfilled in your ears.*

The Holy Spirit constrains the devil. *For the mystery of iniquity doth already work: only he who now letteth will let, until he be taken out of the way* (II Thessalonians 2:7).

After Jesus' crucifixion and resurrection, His apostles carried on the ministry of deliverance and healing:

Acts 3:16, *And his name through faith in his name hath made this man strong, whom ye see and know: yea, the faith which is by him hath given him this perfect soundness in the presence of you all.*

Acts 9:34, *And Peter said unto him, Aeneas, Jesus Christ maketh thee whole: arise, and make thy bed. And he arose immediately.*

Acts 16:18, *And this did she many days. But Paul, being grieved, turned and said to the spirit, I command thee in the name of Jesus Christ to come out of her. And he came out the same hour.*

As successors to the apostles, we are to continue to fight against hell. Jesus' commission to every believer, which is a command, not a suggestion, is found in Mark 16:15-18:

Mark 16:15-18, *And he said unto them, Go ye into all the world, and preach the gospel to every creature.*

v. 16, *He that believeth and is baptized shall be saved; but he that believeth not shall be damned.*

v. 17, *And these signs shall follow them that believe; In my name shall they cast out devils; they shall speak with new tongues;*

v. 18, *They shall take up serpents; and if they drink any deadly thing, it shall not hurt them; they shall lay hands on the sick, and they shall recover.*

SO, WHO IS TO BLAME FOR MAN'S SICKNESS?

There have always been people who blame God for illness, accusing Him of chastening His children with infirmity. For example, Job's comforters thought God was punishing him for his transgressions, but they were wrong (Job 11:13-16).

In John 9, people questioned Jesus as to "who sinned" to cause a man to be born blind. Jesus said that neither the blind man nor his parents were to be blamed:

John 9:1-3, *And as Jesus passed by, he saw a man which was blind from his birth.*
v. 2, *And his disciples asked him, saying, Master, who did sin, this man, or his parents, that he was born blind?*
v. 3, *Jesus answered, Neither hath this man sinned, nor his parents: but that the works of God should be made manifest in him.*

While I was founding a church in Hong Kong, one of the members fell down a flight of stone steps and broke her ankle. One of the other members went to visit her in the hospital. The visitor said, "All right, confess it. Tell me what you have been doing wrong." The injured church member said, "I have not been doing anything wrong." The other argued, "No one would ever fall down a flight of stairs unless there was sin in her life."

As their pastor, it became necessary for me to talk to the Christians and say, "We do not permit the judging of others in our church."

Some sickness is a satanic attack. When Jesus ministered deliverance to the woman bent over with the infirmity for many years, He specifically said that she was bound by Satan.

Actually, the reason for sickness is not nearly as important as understanding that God is both able and willing to heal anyone, regardless of the cause for their sickness.

No one has been called to play God by telling people why they are sick. When we try to explain all of the mysteries surrounding the "why" of human illness, we are going beyond our human disposition. Usually, Jesus did not bother to explain why people were sick. He just healed them. Whatever the cause of a person's illness, it is part of the original curse.

THE TREE OF LIFE

After Adam and Eve ate of the tree of the knowledge of good and evil, not only did they come under a curse, but they were separated from the Tree of Life which held the remedy for the curse.

Genesis 3:24 says, *So he drove out the man; and he placed at the east of the garden of Eden Cherubims, and a flaming sword which turned every way, to keep the way of the tree of life.*

In Revelation 22:2, we learn that the leaves of the Tree of Life were for healing. Man is denied this tree of health and healing, but the cross of Jesus Christ is our Tree of Life.

Ezekiel 47:12 says, *And by the river upon the bank thereof, on this side and on that side, shall grow all trees for meat, whose leaf shall not fade, neither shall the fruit thereof be consumed: it shall bring forth new fruit according to his months, because their waters they issued out of the sanctuary: and the fruit thereof shall be for meat, and the leaf thereof for medicine.*

The first Adam ate the fruit of the forbidden tree and brought sin and sickness into the world. But the last Adam, Jesus Christ, hung on a tree and took sin and sickness out of the world. *Who his own self bare our sins in his own body on the tree, that we, being dead to sins, should live unto righteousness: by whose stripes ye were healed* (I Peter 2:24).

Most people could be healed by themselves if they would put their faith in Jesus Christ of Nazareth and command the devil, "Go! I'm tired of you!" That would be your spirit speaking to your body, telling it to obey, because your spirit is the king of your life as it should be. When your spirit is the king of your life, then your whole body has to follow whether it likes it or not.

As a dominion person, I declare and decree sickness and disease and any symptoms evicted from my life right now, because Jesus bore my sicknesses and diseases and paid the price in full for me to walk in health and wholeness.

-2-

What is Healing?

Jesus Christ has turned the cross, which was the tree of death, into the Tree of Life and blessing. The leaves of this tree heal and bless in every nation where Jesus is preached and received (Revelation 22:2; Matthew 21:22).

Our natural, earthly bodies, which are made of clay, can receive new life, new vigor, and new power. Diseases can be destroyed and maladjustments made right by the power of Jesus Christ.

Physical healing is not wrought by mental powers or psychological therapy. It is not human imagination, nor is it demonic in origin. God, in His mercy, has provided an adequate salvation for the three integral parts of triune man — spirit, soul, and body — through Jesus Christ.

The Bible must be the sole textbook for the subject of divine healing, for man's opinions and ideas bring confusion. The Bible is the Supreme Court of the Christian faith.

THE PRESENT-DAY NEED FOR DIVINE HEALING

Many people in the world are sick. Yet we have more doctors, nurses, hospitals, medical help, scientific discoveries, and inventions than ever before.

People in the world are confused. They do not know whether to trust a medical doctor with his drugs, a surgeon with his scalpel, a psychiatrist with mental analysis, an osteopath or chiropractor readjusting the bones and organs of the body, or if they should just simply trust Jesus. Sickness is a spiritual phenomenon, and we need to deal with it on that basis.

One time when I was at Wheaton College, I stayed in a twin room next to a medical doctor. He said to me, "Sumrall, about 80 to 90 percent of all my patients are sick from the ears up!" I said, "Thank you, doctor."

Isn't that amazing? That means that with most sickness, if you deal with the internal man, the spirit man, you will get to the problem before you get to the exterior of the person, to the fleshly sickness that you are dealing with.

Not only can people be sick in their spirits, they can also be sick in their souls (their mind, will, and emotions). A person who is sick in his mind can be healed, just like a person who is sick in his toe. If God is God, He can heal you, whether it's your spirit, your soul, or your body.

A person whose spirit is crushed and hurt and who has lost his faith in God needs help, and only God can give him that help. Man cannot reach into the interior part of the person and heal him. He can encourage, but only God can do the healing.

I have prayed for many people who were insane, and God healed them. Sometimes insanity is only a possession by an evil spirit, so all you have to do is cast the spirit out, and they are well.

The three parts of man — spirit, soul, and body — are intrinsically integrated together. You cannot separate them. When one area is sick, the other areas also hurt.

Sickness is a form of limited death. Whatever part of you is sick, that part of you is dead and needs resurrection. Christ is that resurrection. He is the only One who can do the healing.

Millions of people are in pain at this very moment. Disease is ravaging the bodies of the old and the young, rich and poor, educated and ignorant, king and slave. Jesus is the Master Physician, and He can heal every kind of disease known among men.

HEALING IS . . .

Let's examine a few descriptions of what healing is:

Healing is divine intervention. Jesus Christ alone is the Healer.

Healing is the recovery from an abnormal physical or emotional aberration.

Man was created to live forever, but the transgression of Adam and Eve opened the door to sickness. In other words, sin was the origination of sickness. With God, man's triunity is one. God equally heals man's spirit, soul, and body.

Healing is a recovery from some kind of sickness or weakness. Sickness is limited death, while health is unlimited life.

Healing is a cure from pain or disability. Jesus said, . . . *They that be whole need not a physician . . .* (Matthew 98:12).

Healing is a restoration to health.

Mark 5:34, *And he said unto her, Daughter, thy faith hath made thee whole; go in peace, and be whole of they plague.*

Healing is victory over the curse.

Luke 13:11, 16, *And, behold, there was a woman which had a spirit of infirmity eighteen years, and was bowed together, and could in no wise lift up herself.*

v. 16, *And ought not this woman, being a daughter of Abraham, whom Satan hath bound, lo, these eighteen years, be loosed from this bond on the sabbath day?*

Matthew 12:22, *Then was brought unto him one possessed with a devil, blind, and dumb: and he healed him, insomuch that the blind and dumb both spake and saw.*

THE CURSE AND THE CURE

There are more sick people in the world today than ever before in history. Those who are sick are not just those in backward, undeveloped nations with poor sanitary conditions, inferior food, and few modern conveniences.

The increase in illness is not limited to areas of overcrowded population, severe climate, or ignorance and superstition. It runs rampant even in the world's so-called "advanced" nations.

Most hospitals are overcrowded, and doctors' offices are jammed with people who are seeking help. Billions of dollars are spent in an effort to get well. Many of the sick get worse and their pain is intensified.

However, the good news is that Jesus Christ came to earth to heal. He was and is the Healer (Acts 10:38). His compassion is the same for the entire world.

Jesus taught us by word and example that there is not a prepackaged routine for receiving healing. He did not anoint everyone with oil; He did not lay hands on everyone; He did not put mud in everybody's eyes. He demonstrated to us that all healing is divine, regardless of the method used.

MY FIRST EXPERIENCES WITH DIVINE HEALING

My Mother Was Healed of Breast Cancer

As an eight-year-old child, one of the first miracles of healing I ever witnessed was that of my own mother who was healed of a very painful breast cancer.

Her doctor of many years said that an attempt to remove the cancer would probably mean that death would come sooner. The doctor dressed the sore and kept it clean, but offered little hope. The pain became so unbearable one night that Mother walked the floor until the early morning hours, crying out to God to relieve her of her torture. It was almost sunrise before she fell exhausted across her bed and went to sleep.

That very morning Mother dreamed that Jesus walked through the door of her bedroom. As He looked at her with great compassion, He reached down and tenderly touched her on the chest. When she awoke, Mother told my unbelieving father about the dream and said that she was going to be healed.

Dad was skeptical. A few days later he asked her, "How is your cancer, dear? You haven't mentioned it lately. Are you suffering much?" Mother answered, "Well, really, I had almost forgotten about the cancer because the pain is gone."

Immediately, Mother went into her bedroom and took off the dressing which covered the malignant sore. To her horror and also to her great joy, there was an awful-looking thing which could best be described as resembling an octopus. It had a center from which several tentacles reached out, and the entire thing was black and ugly in her hand. As she looked down, she noticed that a fine sheen of new baby-pink skin already covered her breast. The cancer had literally dropped off of her body.

Mother lived more than forty years from that day. Cancer never broke out on another place in her body. At the age of eighty-seven, she died peacefully of natural causes.

Grandfather Healed After A Stroke

Another outstanding healing in our family was of my Grandpa Chandler who suffered a stroke while walking downtown one day. He was brought to our house in a pitiful condition; both legs, both arms, his speech, and his bowels were paralyzed.

Mother said that all she knew to do was to call some of the members of her church to come and pray. The rest of the family thought medical help would be better, so they took Grandpa to the hospital.

After the doctor examined him, he turned to Mother and said, "Mrs. Sumrall, your father does not have long in this world. If I were you,

I would take him home and make him as comfortable as possible until the good Lord takes him home."

After that, no one in the family objected to Mother calling in the Christians to pray, because there was nothing else they could do.

It was summertime and all the windows of the house were open, allowing the neighbors to hear. A man named Campbell lived next door, and he claimed to be an infidel. When the praying got loud, he walked over to the fence where my sister was playing and asked, "Louise, what are they trying to do to the old man?" Louise looked up in her childish way and said, "They are praying for Grandpa. He has had a stroke and the doctor said he is going to die, but my mother said that the Lord is going to heal him."

Mr. Campbell laughed and said, "Well, I guess when they are through with him, the old man will be able to jump a ten rail fence." He turned and went back to the rocking chair on the porch.

The next morning when Grandpa awakened, he forgot his paralysis and cried out to my mother, "Betty, Betty, where are my clothes?" "Pa, are you all right?" "Certainly I'm all right," he bellowed. "Didn't you pray for me? Didn't you ask God to give me a miracle?"

Grandpa got up, dressed himself, and walked into the kitchen where he devoured a big breakfast. Then he walked out the back door to inspect the garden. As he did, the man next door called out to my mother from the fence that separated his yard from ours. With tears in his eyes, he apologized for the way he talked to my sister the day before. He confessed that what he had witnessed convinced him that there must indeed be a God who answers prayer.

Weeping almost convulsively, he asked, "Mrs. Sumrall, will you pray for me, that I will come to know God like you do so that when I come to the end, He will accept me as He has accepted you?"

Grandpa lived a strong and vigorous life for thirty-two years after that without ever having another stroke.

Such unmistakable miracles of healing no doubt planted a seed of faith in my youthful heart which would bear fruit in my ministry in years to come.

From the time God first called me to preach as a teenager, I have preached divine healing according to the Bible. God has honored and confirmed His Word as I have seen literally thousands of people healed of every disease and malady imaginable.

The Woman With A New Tongue

One of the most remarkable healings that I have ever known was that of Mrs. Williams, whose tongue was restored after it had been removed at the base because of cancer. For approximately twelve years, Mrs. Williams lived without a tongue and without the ability to speak.

During this time, she raised two daughters. She communicated with her husband, children, and neighbors by writing on a pad which she always kept with her. In the town of Walstow, Mrs. Williams was well-known to hundreds of people as "the woman without a tongue."

One night she attended a revival meeting in her city. Mrs. Williams had a bad cold that night, so she went up to have the evangelist pray for her. When the evangelist asked, "What do you want?" she suddenly realized that she had left her pad and pencil back at her seat and was unable to tell him. Pointing to her throat was all she could do.

Laying hands upon her head, the evangelist prayed, "O God, give this lady the desire of her heart." As he prayed, Mrs. Williams began to choke. Something began to move in the back of her throat. Right there on the platform, a new tongue formed within a few minutes. She began to speak, to the delight and amazement of the local citizens who knew her.

This miracle of healing involved a creative act of God almost beyond human comprehension. The fascinating thing about it to me was that when Mrs. Williams would open her mouth, you could clearly see where the old flesh and the new joined. It was as if they had been welded together.

As she told her story and showed her tongue to the people in my crusades throughout England, great faith was born in the people's hearts to believe God for personal miracles.

God's power, might, and creativity reside within me through the Holy Spirit. I am walking in divine health in every area of my life. Thank you, Jesus, that you are the same yesterday, today, and forever! What you did yesterday, you will do today!

-3-

Biblical Reasons for Illness

Obedience to the full counsel of God's Word will alert you to avoid the traps that Satan sets to ensnare you with sickness and disease. The light of the Word in you will drive out Satan's darkness (Deuteronomy 28:15; Proverbs 4:18-27; John 10:10; I John 3:8; Galatians 3:13).

We have already established that sickness and disease entered mankind because of the transgression of Adam and Eve (Genesis 3:1-3), and that Satan is the author of sickness and disease. We have established that sickness is satanic oppression (Acts 10:38).

Now, let's examine some biblical reasons as to "how" Satan is able to bring sickness and disease into a person's life.

1. Disrespect for God and/or His anointed

An example of this "open door" into a person's life is found in Numbers 21:6-9:

Numbers 21:6-9, *And the LORD sent fiery serpents among the people, and they bit the people; and much people of Israel died.*

v. 7, *Therefore the people came to Moses, and said, We have sinned, for we have spoken against the LORD, and*

against thee; pray unto the LORD, that he
take away the serpents from us. And Moses
prayed for the people.

v. 8, *And the LORD said unto Moses,
Make thee a fiery serpent, and set it upon
a pole: and it shall come to pass, that every one that is bitten, when he looketh upon
it, shall live.*

v. 9, *And Moses made a serpent of
brass, and put it upon a pole, and it came
to pass, that if a serpent had bitten any man,
when he beheld the serpent of brass, he
lived.*

In John 3:14 Jesus said, *And as Moses lifted
up the serpent in the wilderness, even so must
the Son of man be lifted up.* When the Israelites
looked upon the serpent God had provided for
them, representative of the Lord Jesus Christ in
the New Testament, they received healing from
rebellion and sin. Those who refused to look
upon the serpent died.

**2. Wrong activities and habits can be an
open door to sickness and disease.**

Many sicknesses are caused by the way
people live: improper diet, lack of exercise, lack
of proper rest, worry, and fear.

God expects us to give our bodies time to
recuperate if we want to use them for his Kingdom and for His glory. There should be proper
diet, exercise, and rest.

We understand from medical science that worry can cause physical illness. If you are greatly disturbed inside, it will manifest in some sort of sickness or disease. Take your cares to Jesus and leave them there!

3. Some sicknesses and diseases are hereditary.

You need not have weakness or sickness in your body because your father or mother had a malfunction in any part of their body or mind. Regardless of what your grandma, grandpa, aunt, uncle, mama, or daddy had, you can be healed of any kind of disease.

There are people who expect to die at the same age their father was when he died. If he died at age forty-seven, when they reach forty-six and a half, they start making a box to crawl into.

I don't believe you have to carry anything that was before you, so if you think you have some kind of hereditary problem, drop the problem. Let Jesus Christ take care of it, because He is abundantly able to heal you.

4. Some sicknesses and diseases are directly related to satanic operation.

We saw this with the woman who had a spirit of infirmity for eighteen years.

In Matthew 17:14-18, Jesus *rebuked the devil* in a child who was *lunatic, and sore vexed* (v. 15). Verse 18 says, *And Jesus rebuked the devil; and he departed out of him: and the child was cured from that very hour.*

Notice, Jesus did not pray for this child. He rebuked the devil, the devil departed, and the child was healed.

I believe the reason medical science can't touch a great percentage of our illnesses today is because they are spiritual.

A woman came into my office who had spent thousands of dollars searching for a diagnosis and remedy for pain she was experiencing in her head, chest, and the organs of her body, and a severe burning sensation in various parts of her body. Doctors could find nothing wrong with her.

As I talked to her, I saw that her symptoms were not physical. That's why the doctors could not find the cause. I cast that thing out of her, and she has never had it since.

5. Sickness can be caused by transgression.

Sickness can be directly related to coming against God or rebelling against Him.

Deuteronomy 28:1, 15 says:

Deuteronomy 28:1, *And it shall come to pass, if thou shalt hearken diligently unto the voice of the LORD thy God, to observe and to do all his commandments which I command thee this day, that the LORD thy*

God will set thee on high above all nations of the earth:

    v. 15, *But it shall come to pass, if thou wilt not hearken unto the voice of the LORD thy God, to observe to do all his commandments and his statutes which I command thee this day; that all these curses shall come upon thee, and overtake thee.*

6. Sickness and disease can be caused by covetousness.

Malachi 3:8-9 says:

    Malachi 3:8-9, *Will a man rob God? Yet ye have robbed me. But ye say, Wherein have we robbed thee? In tithes and offerings.*

    v. 9, *Ye are cursed with a curse: for ye have robbed me, even this whole nation.*

    I Timothy 6:6-10 says:

    I Timothy 6:6-10, *But godliness with contentment is great gain.*

    v. 7, *For we brought nothing into this world, and it is certain we can carry nothing out.*

    v. 8, *And having food and raiment let us be therewith content.*

    v. 9, *But they that will be rich fall into temptation and a snare, and into many fool-*

ish and hurtful lusts, which drown men in destruction and perdition.

v. 10, *For the love of money is the root of all evil: which while some coveted after, they have erred from the faith, and pierced themselves through with many sorrows.*

Many people are ill today because they have been unfair to God and haven't given to Him what belongs to Him. The Gospel can only go out over the world as people love it and give toward it. God can do nothing outside of your liberality.

7. Immorality is an open door to sickness and disease.

I Corinthians 6:18 says,

I Corinthians 6:18, *Flee fornication. Every sin that a man doeth is without the body; but he that committeth fornication sinneth against his own body.*

I Thessalonians 4:3-7 says:

I Thessalonians 4:3-7, *For this is the will of God, even your sanctification, that ye should abstain from fornication:*

v. 4, *That every one of you should know how to possess his vessel in sanctification and honour;*

v. 5, *Not in the lust of concupiscence, even as the Gentiles which know not God:*

v. 6, *That no man go beyond and de-fraud his brother in any matter: because that the Lord is the avenger of all such, as we also have forewarned you and testified.*

v. 7, *For God hath not called us unto uncleanness, but unto holiness."*

Many people are going through agony and many homes have been busted to pieces because of venereal diseases which have been the result of immorality. I want to assure you, a clean life is the best life.

8. Unforgiveness and resentment are open doors for sickness and disease.

Matthew 6:14-15 says,

Matthew 6:14-15, *For if ye forgive men their trespasses, your heavenly Father will also forgive you:*

v. 15, *But if ye forgive not men their trespasses, neither will your Father forgive your trespasses.*

Hebrews 12:5-8 says:

Hebrews 12:5-8, *And ye have forgotten the exhortation which speaketh unto you as unto children, My son, despise not thou the chastening of the Lord, nor faint when thou art rebuked of him:*

v. 6, *For whom the Lord loveth he chasteneth, and scourgeth every son whom he receiveth.*

v. 7, *If ye endure chastening, God dealeth with you as with sons; for what son is he whom the father chasteneth not?*

v. 8, *But if ye be without chastisement, whereof all are partakers, then are ye bastards, and not sons.*

Unforgiveness and resentment can cause disease and will keep you from receiving from God.

9. Fear is an open door for sickness and disease to walk into your life.

Job said, *For the thing which I greatly feared is come upon me, and that which I was afraid of is come unto me* (Job 3:25).

I John 4:18 says, *There is no fear in love; but perfect love casteth out fear: because fear hath torment. He that feareth is not made perfect in love.*

Fear dominates the lives of many people. If you are afraid you are going to get sick, you will. If you are afraid you are going to catch something, you will. Fear should not have any part or parcel in the way we live.

At seventeen years of age, I was full of fear. Lying on the floor weeping and trembling, God spoke to me, "Read Isaiah 41:10-11." I picked up my Bible and read:

Isaiah 41:10-11, *Fear thou not; for I am with thee: be not dismayed; for I am thy God: I will strengthen thee; yea, I will help thee; yea, I will uphold thee with the right hand of my righteousness.*

v. 11, *Behold, all they that were incensed against thee shall be ashamed and confounded: they shall be as nothing; and they that strive with thee shall perish.*

As I read these verses, I felt God reach down inside of me and pull something out, and I have never been tormented with fear from that day to this.

10. The worship of idols can bring human illness.

In Exodus 20:4-6, God says:

Exodus 20:4-6, *Thou shalt not make unto thee any graven image, or any likeness of any thing that is in heaven above, or that is in the earth beneath, or that is in the water under the earth:*

v. 5, *Thou shalt not bow down thyself to them, nor serve them: for I the LORD thy God am a jealous God, visiting the iniquity of the fathers upon the children unto the third and fourth generation of them that hate me;*

v. 6, *And showing mercy unto thousands of them that love me, and keep my commandments.*

11. The wrong use of communion can be an open door for sickness and disease to come into your life.

I Corinthians 11:30-32 says:

I Corinthians 11:30-32, *For this cause many are weak and sickly among you, and many sleep.*

v. 31, *For if we would judge ourselves, we should not be judged.*

v. 32, *But when we are judged, we are chastened of the Lord, that we should not be condemned with the world.*

I attend to God's Word daily by reading, studying, meditating upon it, and obeying it, for it is life and health to me in spirit, soul, and body. I have been redeemed from the curse of the law so I can walk in newness of life and bring heaven to earth in my life and in the lives of others who will believe and receive Jesus Christ into their hearts and lives.

-4-

The Healing Covenant

When you are born again, you enter into covenant agreement with God. Everything that He is and everything that He has becomes yours as you yield (or surrender) yourself completely to Him. Healing and divine life are part of your inheritance in this life through Jesus Christ (Exodus 15:26; Matthew 8:17).

A covenant is an agreement between two parties; a binding and solemn vow; a corporate resolution. It literally means to come together. It is a mutual understanding between two parties, each binding to the other to fulfill certain obligations.

God made a covenant or contract with the nation of Israel, which was vital to their well-being. His mighty hand of power delivered them from Egypt and King Pharaoh. By omnipotence He opened up the Red Sea. Three days out in the wilderness, God made a divine healing covenant with His people. This covenant was an essential part of their redemption.

Israel came to the waters of Marah, but found the waters to be bitter. The whole nation feared that they would perish from thirst. God directed Moses to cut and cast a certain tree into the waters. This, no doubt, was a type of the cross, for the waters became sweet. Healing has always been related to a tree.

Exodus 15:23-25 says:

Exodus 15:23-25, *And when they came to Marah, they could not drink of the waters of Marah, for they were bitter: therefore the name of it was called Marah.*
v. 24, *And the people murmured against Moses, saying, What shall we drink?*
v. 25, *And he cried unto the LORD; and the LORD showed him a tree, which when he had cast into the waters, the waters were made sweet: there he made for them a statute and an ordinance, and there he proved them.*

In John 4:13-14 Jesus spoke of the "living water" that He provides, which springs up into everlasting life:

John 4:13-14, *Jesus answered and said unto her, Whosoever drinketh of this water shall thirst again:*
v. 14, *But whosoever drinketh of the water that I shall give him shall never thirst; but the water that I shall give him shall be in him a well of water springing up into everlasting life.*

God could have healed once, or even occasionally, but instead He bound Himself by His own Word with a covenant to constantly and faithfully heal His people of their diseases. He is "the Lord that healeth thee."

THE COVENANT SPEAKS TO US OF RESPONSIBILITY

The covenant of Exodus 15:25-26 was sacred and binding. Our responsibilities are stated in verse 26, . . . *If thou wilt diligently hearken to the voice of the LORD thy God, and wilt do that which is right in his sight, and wilt give ear to his commandments, and keep all his statutes . . . .*

When our responsibilities are met, God's healing covenant is enforced: . . . *I will put none of these diseases upon thee, which I have brought upon the Egyptians: for I am the Lord that healeth thee* (v. 26). If you study this carefully, you can see how living right keeps you healthy. Living for God brings health to the bones as well as to the spirit.

Jehovah Rapha is one of the great, distinctive, redemptive names of God. It reveals His healing nature, His integrity, and His personality.

Other areas of responsibility we are to fulfill in the healing covenant include:

1. Confessing our faults one to another

James 5:16, *Confess your faults one to another, and pray one for another, that ye may be healed. The effectual fervent prayer of a righteous man availeth much.*

In the contract we have with God, His Word says that if we've got a problem or a sin, we must confess it and get it out so that we can be healed.

An interesting situation took place at a hospital in our city. I read a slip of paper containing a prayer request, put it in my pocket, and rushed over to the hospital. I went to room 512, although I later discovered that I was to go to 412.

Being in a hurry, I got off the elevator, ran into room 512 and the first man I saw I asked, "Do you need prayer?" He said, "Yes." So I proceeded to pray a real victorious prayer for him. When I got through he said, "Who are you?" I said, "In that case, who are you?" He said, "I am Father So-and-so from Notre Dame." I said, "I am Lester Sumrall from the other end of town." Then he began to cry.

He said, "I have prayed for hours that if there was anybody in this city who could pray, for God to send him to me." He said, "When you came through that door, I knew God had sent you."

I reached into my pocket and said, "I'm on the wrong floor." "No," he said, "you're not, you're on the right floor!" If a person has been praying, God will cause you to miss a floor to get to him!

2. Forgiving, having no resentment or guilt

Matthew 18:15, *Moreover if thy brother shall trespass against thee, go and tell him his fault between thee and him alone: if he shall hear thee, thou hast gained thy brother.*

3. Loving God before men

Isaiah 59:1-2, *Behold, the LORD'S hand is not shortened, that it cannot save; neither his ear heavy, that it cannot hear:*

v. 2, *But your iniquities have separated between you and your God, and your sins have hid his face from you, that he will not hear.*

4. Confessing the sins of your nation

II Chronicles 7:14, *If my people, which are called by my name, shall humble themselves, and pray, and seek my face, and turn from their wicked ways; then will I hear from heaven, and will forgive their sin, and will heal their land.*

THE COVENANT EMBODIES THREE MAIN OBJECTIVES

First, when a person is sick, he can have divine healing administered through the proper spiritual channels. The second, covering greater miracles, is divine health. It is more wonderful for plagues not to come near your dwelling. And third, divine life, the union of soul and spirit between God and man, causes man to be the recipient of God's life and nature.

GOD NEVER RETROGRESSES

We are not living on the leftovers of yesterday's feast. Anything that God did for your grandma, He will do for you, maybe even a little better because He never retrogresses. He cannot go backwards. The healing covenant is still in force. Christ *". . . Himself took our infirmities, and bare our sicknesses"* (Matthew 8:17).

The writer of Hebrews speaks of a better hope, a better testament, a better covenant:

Hebrews 7:19, *For the law made nothing perfect, but the bringing in of a better hope did; by the which we draw nigh unto God.*

Hebrews 7:22, *By so much was Jesus made a surety of a better testament.*

Hebrews 8:6, *But now hath he obtained a more excellent ministry, by how much also he is the mediator of a better covenant, which was established upon better promises.*

God is truly doing more on the face of the earth at this moment than ever before.

Your relationship with healing is not an incident. It is a covenant. God cannot break His Word. He honors His Word above His name (Psalm 138:2), and we stand upon His covenant promises.

I am a covenant partner with God. His divine life is mine, not only in the area of health, but in every area of my life. His mercies and compassion are new to me every morning according to Lamentations 3:22-23.

-5-

Why Some People Are Not Healed

We receive healing, not by any merit of our own, but because Jesus, in His great love, purchased healing for us on Calvary (Job 3:25; Luke 13:10, 16).

I believe in health for every person who loves God, but the devil does not want you to have health. There must be a resistance to the devil against sickness.

The devil has no record of healing people. Search his fingerprints throughout history and you will find him stealing, killing, and destroying (John 10:10).

There are "worldly wise men" who are actually jealous of God because they cannot explain healing naturally. In fact, a miracle is embarrassing to them. Colossians 2:8 warns us, *Beware lest any man spoil you through philosophy and vain deceit, after the tradition of men, after the rudiments of the world, and not after Christ.*

The traditions of some "religious leaders" are contrary to truth. In Matthew 15:3, Jesus challenged the scribes and Pharisees with this question, *Why do ye also transgress the commandment of God by your tradition?*

Remember, it was the religious leaders who persecuted Jesus and had Him put to death.

The scribes and Pharisees taught those who followed them, but they taught them incorrectly. Jesus said, *Woe unto you, scribes and Pharisees, hypocrites! for ye compass sea and land to make one proselyte, and when he is made, ye make him twofold more the child of hell than yourselves* (Matthew 23:15).

HINDRANCES TO HEALING

Not everyone who hears God's salvation plan is born again. Likewise, not everyone who is prayed for to receive healing is healed. Let's identify some of the things that keep people from receiving their healing.

1. Some people have not prepared their hearts to receive their deliverance and healing.

They do not take time in the Word of God. If I needed a healing, I would read about fifty promises of healing and get them bubbling down inside of me. Search the scriptures. Romans 10:17 says, *So then faith cometh by hearing, and hearing by the word of God*.

Fast and pray. In every instance where I have interceded for a terrible case of demon possession, I have fasted and prayed beforehand. I fast to prepare myself in my spirit. I refuse food for my body. I tell my soulical parts to lie down in peace. My spiritual being becomes strong by reading the Word and praying.

When you want something from God, pre-pare yourself to receive it.

2. Some people are not healed because of doubt and unbelief.

There were few healings in Nazareth, Jesus' hometown, because of unbelief. *And he [Jesus] could there do no mighty work, save that he laid his hands upon a few sick folk, and healed them* (Mark 6:5).

3. Some people do not receive their healing because of uncertainty.

Some people are not certain that it is the will of God for them to be healed. If you do not accept the fact that it is the will of God for you to be healed, you will find it difficult to receive healing. These same people will take medicine. My question is, "If it is not the will of God for you to be healed, why are you working against God's will in order to get healed?"

4. Some people are not healed because they try to receive through their human "goodness."

If you come to the Lord and tell Him how good you are and that you ought to be healed because of your goodness, you have missed the whole plan and purpose of redemption. We are healed by the sufferings of Jesus Christ. Isaiah 53:5 says, . . . *with his stripes we are healed.*

5. Unconfessed sin in a person's life will keep him from receiving healing.

James 5:16 says, *Confess your faults one*

to another, and pray one for another, that ye
may be healed.* Sickness could be the result of
hidden sin in a person's life. You must be willing to confess it and forsake it. David said, *If I
regard iniquity in my heart, the Lord will not
hear me* (Psalm 66:18).

**6. Some people are not healed because
they defile their bodies.**

Alcohol, tobacco, and illicit sex are some
of the things that defile your body. Scripture says
that . . . *your body is the temple of the Holy
Ghost* (I Corinthians 6:19). God does not oper-
ate a charity hospital for the devil. If you wish
to be healed, then go and sin no more (John
5:14).

**7. An unforgiving spirit will keep some
people from being healed.**

If you have an unforgiving spirit, are stub-
born, or you have bitterness toward someone,
then you will not be able to receive the kind of
healing that you want the Lord to give you.

Jesus said in Matthew 5:23-24:

Matthew 5:23-24, *Therefore if thou
bring thy gift to the altar, and there
rememberest that thy brother hath ought
against thee;*

v. 24, *Leave there thy gift before the
altar, and go thy way; first be reconciled
to thy brother, and then come and offer
thy gift.*

8. Some people are not healed because they never set a certain time for their healing.

In my experience, I have found that people are not healed because they do not set a moment for their healing. If you say, "Sometime in the indefinite future God is going to heal me," that is forever! Jesus said, *Therefore I say unto you, What things soever ye desire, when ye pray, believe that ye receive them, and ye shall have them* (Mark 11:24).

There has to be a point of contact. The little woman with the issue of blood who came to Jesus said, *If I may but touch his garment, I shall be whole* (Matthew 9:21). She had twelve years of sickness in her body, but she set a specific moment of contact and said, "I shall be healed at that moment."

9. Some sickness is not related to you but is a direct attack of the devil.

In speaking of the woman with the spirit of infirmity for eighteen years, Jesus said, . . . *this woman . . . whom Satan hath bound . . .* (Luke 13:16).

Job was a good man, but he lost his home, his children, and his health through the devil's attack.

Remember, the devil can only go so far. We can put him to flight. The trial of your faith will win (Job 42:10).

DELAY IS NOT DENIAL!

In Acts 3, there was a man at the Beautiful Gate who had lain there for many years. Entering Jerusalem, Jesus' clothes must have brushed him a dozen times or more, yet Jesus never healed him. However, when Peter and John came by the Beautiful Gate, he was healed. Five thousand men, plus women and children, were saved that day as a result of his healing.

If Jesus had healed this man, He would have been called "Beelzebub," and the healed man would have been thrown out of the synagogue. He would have lost his membership in the church because the "religious" folk hated Jesus. When Peter and John touched this man, he was healed through Jesus' power. His healing brought tremendous glory to the Kingdom of God.

I think of how God delivered and healed Clarita Villanueva in the Philippines of the demon spirit that was hurting her. Thousands have been blessed by her testimony.

When you receive a healing, you ought to broadcast it to the world!

I hunger and thirst for God's Word more than for natural food for my body. I keep myself built up in God's Word so I am strong in Him and in the power of His might. It is in Jesus Christ that I live and move and have my being according to Acts 17:28.

-6-

Healing Throughout the Bible

The Bible is a living miracle in literature. The Bible has 66 miracle books blending themselves into one whole. Each book teaches the wholeness of man.

There are those who believe that the message of healing is an isolated doctrine and that it is not related to the covenant of God and to your own salvation.

Dr. Lillian Yoeman says, "I was healed by the whole Bible. The Bible is a great mass of healing power for all men."

I have chosen healing verses from every book of the Bible to show you that God wants you well spiritually, emotionally, and physically.

Make the Word work in your life!

Old Testament

Divine Healing is taught in every
book of the Old Testament.

1. GENESIS

God created man in His likeness and image, free from physical disabilities. Man was created a well person and not designed for sickness, but was meant to have health and joy. Whatever we lack in ourselves, He will provide.

Our God is Jehovah-Jireh, which means "the Lord will provide" (Genesis 22:8).

Genesis 1:27, *So God created man in his own image, in the image of God created he him; male and female created he them.*

2. EXODUS

The Israelites were God's chosen people. Three million of them wandered in the wilderness for forty years, but there was not one feeble person among their tribes (Psalm 105:37). He is Jehovah-Rapha, "The Lord will heal."

Exodus 15:26, . . . *If thou wilt diligently hearken to the voice of the LORD thy God, and wilt do that which is right in his sight, and wilt give ear to his commandments, and keep all his statutes, I will put none of these diseases upon thee, which I have brought upon the Egyptians: for I am the LORD that healeth thee.*

3. LEVITICUS

A person who had leprosy was pronounced unclean and isolated from the rest of the people because of the danger of transmitting the disease to others. Even his house could be infected. However, there was hope: even the lepers could be cleansed.

Leviticus 14:48, *And if the priest shall come in, and look upon it, and, behold, the plague hath not spread in the house, after the house was plastered: then the priest shall pronounce the house clean, because the plague is healed.*

4. NUMBERS

In the book of Numbers, every sickness was dealt with supernaturally. Everyone who had been bitten by a serpent was healed when he looked upon the brass serpent which Moses built. It was a type of the Lord Jesus Christ on the cross, from whom we can receive life and health when bitten by sin. It's God's healing power in action.

Numbers 21:9, *And Moses made a serpent of brass, and put it upon a pole, and it came to pass, that if a serpent had bitten any man, when he beheld the serpent of brass, he lived.*

5. DEUTERONOMY

God promised to take away all sickness from His people who will love and follow the Lord their God. There is healing for every disease known to man.

Deuteronomy 7:15, *And the LORD will take away from thee all sickness, and will put none of the evil diseases of Egypt, which thou knowest, upon thee; but will lay them upon all them that hate thee.*

6. JOSHUA

Caleb, at 85 years of age, was as strong and healthy as a man of 40. He wanted to be a general and had picked out a mountain that he intended to possess. God had preserved him in perfect health during 45 years in the wilderness. Divine health is even better than healing.

Joshua 14:10-11, *And now, behold, the LORD hath kept me alive, as he said, these forty and five years, even since the LORD spake this word unto Moses, while the children of Israel wandered in the wilder-ness: and now, lo, I am this day fourscore and five years old.*

v. 11, *As yet I am as strong this day as I was in the day that Moses sent me: as my strength was then, even so is my strength now, for war, both to go out, and to come in.*

7. JUDGES

In the generations of war and blood that the people of Israel went through, they began to realize that the Lord could be their peace. You cannot have a healthy body with a disturbed inner man. Jehovah-Shalom, "the Lord our peace," gives tranquility to our spirit, soul, and body.

Judges 6:23-24, *And the LORD said unto* (Gideon) *him, Peace be unto thee; fear not: thou shalt not die.*

v. 24, *Then Gideon built an altar there unto the LORD, and called it Jehovah-sha-lom.*

8. RUTH

Ruth healed the spirit of Naomi, her mother-in-law. She was grieved and depressed over the death of her husband and two sons. It is just as important to get your spirit healed as it is to get your body healed.

Ruth 1:20, *And she said unto them, Call me not Naomi, call me Mara: for the Al-mighty hath dealt very bitterly with me.*

Ruth 4:14, *And the women said unto Naomi, Blessed be the LORD, which hath not left thee this day without a kinsman, that his name may be famous in Israel.*

9. I SAMUEL

Hannah was not able to have children. It was a disgrace for a woman not to have children in those days, so she prayed desperately, asking the Lord to have mercy on her. A year later, Samuel was born. He later became a mighty prophet in Israel.

I Samuel 1:11, *And she vowed a vow, and said, O Lord of hosts, if thou wilt indeed look on the affliction of thine handmaid, and remember me, and not forget thine handmaid, but wilt give unto thine handmaid a man child, then I will give him unto the Lord all the days of his life, and there shall no razor come upon his head.*

10. II SAMUEL

Sometimes a whole nation can be healed because of the prayers of God's people. David interceded for Israel and the entire nation was healed of a great epidemic.

II Samuel 24:25, *And David built there an altar unto the LORD, and offered burnt offerings and peace offerings. So the LORD was intreated for the land and the plague was stayed from Israel.*

11. I KINGS

King Solomon prayed a tremendous prayer for the entire nation at the dedication of the Temple. His prayer was that any time the people of Israel called upon Jehovah for healing or any other need, God would hear and answer.

I Kings 8:37-39, *If there be in the land famine, if there be pestilence, blasting, mildew, locust, or if there be caterpiller; if their* enemy besiege them in the land of their cities; whatsoever plague, whatsoever sickness there be;

v. 38, *What prayer and supplication soever be made by any man, or by all thy people Israel, which shall know every man the plague of his own heart, and spread forth his hands toward this house:*

v. 39, *Then hear thou in heaven thy dwelling place, and forgive, and do, and give to every man according to his ways, whose heart thou knowest; (for thou, even thou only, knowest the hearts of all the children of men;)*

12. II KINGS

The power of God to heal is not just limited to sickness. Jesus Christ is the resurrection and the life, and at times people have even been raised from the dead. That was the case when Elisha raised a boy from the dead. Prayer and breathing into his mouth brought him back to life.

II Kings 4:32-35, *And when Elisha was come into the house, behold, the child was dead, and laid upon his bed.*

v. 33, *He went in therefore, and shut the door upon them twain, and prayed unto the Lord.*

v. 34, *And he went up, and lay upon the child, and put his mouth upon his mouth, and his eyes upon his eyes, and his hands upon his hands: and he stretched himself upon the child; and the flesh of the child waxed warm.*

v. 35, *Then he returned, and walked in the house to and fro; and went up, and stretched himself upon him: and the child sneezed seven times, and the child opened his eyes.*

13. I CHRONICLES

The Lord protected and preserved David through many battles. God is able to not only heal us from sickness and protect in danger, He can also keep us from sickness and calamities. God is Jehovah-Nissi, which means "God our banner."

I Chronicles 18:6, *Then David put garrisons in Syria-damascus; and the Syrians became David's servants, and brought gifts. Thus the LORD preserved David whithersoever he went.*

14. II CHRONICLES

In II Chronicles, we have a contrast between two kings, Asa and Hezekiah. Hezekiah sought the Lord when he was sick and was healed. Asa, on the other hand, refused to seek the Lord and went to the physicians instead. The Bible stated he died. I don't believe it was because he went to the physicians, but he defied the Lord when he openly refused to consult Him.

II Chronicles 16:12-13, *And Asa in the thirty and ninth year of his reign was diseased in his feet, until his disease was exceeding great: yet in his disease he sought not to the LORD, but to the physicians.*

v. 13, *And Asa slept with his fathers, and died in the one and fortieth year of his reign.*

15. EZRA

The Lord healed the spirits of a discouraged nation. He revived Israel in their bondage and gave them "a nail in his holy place." A nail will lift up, keep in place and sustain an object. God Himself was a nail of healing and strength to His people.

Ezra 9:8, *And now for a little space grace hath been shewed from the LORD our God, to leave us a remnant to escape, and to give us a nail in his holy place, that our God may lighten our eyes, and give us a little reviving in our bondage.*

16. NEHEMIAH

There is healing and vitality in joy. The joy of the Lord even brings physical strength and a merry heart is like medicine.

Nehemiah 8:10, *Then he said unto them, Go your way, eat the fat, and drink the sweet, and send portions unto them for whom nothing is prepared: for this day is holy unto our LORD: neither be ye sorry; for the joy of the LORD is your strength.*

17. ESTHER

Circumstances of life can bring sorrow into your life. Sorrow is a sickness, but Jesus wants to be your burden-bearer. When healing and divine provisions come to you, sorrow goes away. Queen Esther and the Jews in Persia experienced deliverance and their mourning was turned into joy.

Esther 9:22, *As the days wherein the Jews rested from their enemies, and the month which was turned unto them from sorrow to joy, and from mourning into a good day: that they should make them days of feasting and joy, and of sending portions one to another, and gifts to the poor.*

18. JOB

God is gracious and He will give you strength and deliverance when you feel yourself slipping into a pit. We have a ransom and that ransom is, of course, the Lord Jesus Christ.

Job 33:24, *Then he is gracious unto him, and saith, Deliver him from going down to the pit; I have found a ransom.*

19. PSALMS

The Psalms are full of Scriptures and healing. God has great pity for those who are sick, or hurt, or who need strength from Him. The Word of God is what delivers us.

Psalm 103:13, *Like as a father pitieth his children, so the LORD pitieth them that fear him.*

Psalm 107:20, *He sent his word, and healed them, and delivered them from their destructions.*

Psalm 23:1, *The LORD is my shepherd; I shall not want.*

20. PROVERBS

The Word instructs us, not only how we can be healed, but also tells us how we can stay well. Solomon tells his son to heed his words and to follow his advice.

Proverbs 4:20, 22, *My son, attend to my words; incline thine ear unto my sayings.*

v. 22, *For they are life unto those that find them, and health to all their flesh.*

21. ECCLESIASTES

The time to be healed is when you are sick. We have a right to say, "God, heal me." His healing power can be yours in Jesus' name.

Ecclesiastes 3:1, 3, *To every thing there is a season, and a time to every purpose under the heaven:*

v. 3, . . . *and a time to heal . . .*

22. SONG OF SOLOMON

Song of Solomon 6:10 speaks of a type of the Church of the Lord Jesus Christ. The Church cannot be as ". . . terrible as an army with banners . . ." if it is sick and afflicted, or if it is cast down and defeated in spirit. The Church receives its strength and vitality from God, and so does the individual Christian.

Song of Solomon 6:10, *Who is she that looketh forth as the morning, fair as the moon, clear as the sun, and terrible as an army with banners?*

23. ISAIAH

Isaiah speaks about the power of God to heal, bless, strengthen, and increase. This can be a promise for couples who cannot have children in the natural. God can heal the womb. It can also be applied spiritually where we can become fruitful and multiply as a Christian.

Isaiah 54:1, 3, *Sing, O barren, thou that didst not bear; break forth into singing, and cry aloud, thou that didst not travail with child: for more are the children of the deso-*

late than the children of the married wife, saith the LORD.

v. 3, *For thou shalt break forth on the right hand and on the left; and thy seed shall inherit the Gentiles, and make the desolate cities to be inhabited.*

24. JEREMIAH

The Lord promises safety and restoration to His people. He will restore health and heal wounds. Those filled with grief can experience healing in every part of their total being.

Jeremiah 30:17, *For I will restore health unto thee, and I will heal thee of thy wounds, saith the LORD; because they called thee an Outcast, saying, This is Zion, whom no man seeketh after.*

25. LAMENTATIONS

Affliction does not come from God. He does not make you sick, nor does He want you to be sick. God is a giver of life. Many times sickness comes to us through bad living habits, or unbelief. May God help us to retain within us the mighty powers of the living God to be what He would have us to be.

Lamentations 3:33, *For he doth not afflict willingly nor grieve the children of men.*

26. EZEKIEL

Ezekiel called the city Jehovah-Shamah, which means "the Lord is there." Wherever the Lord is, there is healing, there is health, there is power, and there is truth.

Ezekiel 48:35, *It was round about eighteen thousand measures: and the name of the city from that day shall be, The LORD is there.*

27. DANIEL

Daniel, Hananiah, Mishael, and Azariah ate only vegetables and water, while the other Hebrew slaves ate from the king's table. Because these boys were putting God first in their lives, He made them brighter and healthier looking than all the other children. Even if we only have bread and water to eat, God can give added strength and life.

Daniel 1:15, *And at the end of ten days their countenances appeared fairer and fatter in flesh than all the children which did eat the portion of the king's meat.*

28. HOSEA

It is possible to be healed, yet not recognize the Healer. Many people do not know what God can do for them, they do not know how much He loves them or that He wishes to help them.

Hosea 11:3, *I taught Ephraim also to go, taking them by their arms; but they knew not that I healed them.*

29. JOEL

God can not only heal you, but He can heal the land in which you live. What the devil may have destroyed, God can restore to you again.

Joel 2:25, *And I will restore to you the years that the locust hath eaten, the cankerworm, and the caterpiller, and the palmerworm, my great army which I sent among you.*

30. AMOS

The secret to a successful and pros-perous life is to seek the Lord and to keep His commandments.

Amos 5:4, *For thus saith the LORD unto the house of Israel, Seek ye me, and ye shall live.*

31. OBADIAH

God wants to deliver us from bondage so we can live holy and righteous lives. He said that then shall the "house of Jacob possess their possessions."

Obadiah 17, *But upon mount Zion shall be deliverance, and there shall be holiness; and the house of Jacob shall possess their possessions.*

32. JONAH

The Lord preserved Jonah from drowning. When he was ready to surrender to the will of God, he came forth from that ordeal a healthy person and a preacher of the Gospel.

Jonah 1:17, *Now the LORD had prepared a great fish to swallow up Jonah. And Jonah was in the belly of the fish three days and three nights.*

33. MICAH

Sickness is a result of sin. We can transgress against spiritual or physical laws. When we get rid of transgression, we can have health.

Micah 6:13, *Therefore also will I make thee sick in smiting thee, in making thee desolate because of thy sins.*

34. NAHUM

God will not heal you if you live a wicked life. You need to repent and change your wicked ways before God will hear your prayer.

Nahum 3:19, *There is no healing of thy bruise; thy wound is grievous: all that hear the bruit of thee shall clap the hands over thee: for upon whom hath not thy wickedness passed continually?*

35. HABAKKUK

The Lord makes our step light and swift. He fills us with joy and strength.

Habakkuk 3:19, *The LORD God is my strength, and he will make my feet like hinds' feet, and he will make me to walk upon mine high places. To the chief singer on my stringed instruments.*

36. ZEPHANIAH

Even when we are afflicted and poor in the eyes of the world, we are strong when we put our trust in the Lord. We can use the name of Jesus, a name that is above every other name.

Zephaniah 3:12, *I will also leave in the midst of thee an afflicted and poor people, and they shall trust in the name of the LORD.*

37. HAGGAI

Strength comes from having the Lord present with you.

Haggai 2:4, *Yet now be strong, O Zerubbabel, saith the LORD; and be strong, O Joshua, son of Josedech, the high priest; and be strong, all ye people of the land, saith the LORD, and work: for I am with you, saith the LORD of hosts.*

38. ZECHARIAH
Disobedience prevents healing.

Zechariah 11:16, *For, lo, I will raise up a shepherd in the land, which shall not visit those that be cut off, neither shall seek the young one, nor heal that that is broken, nor feed that that standeth still: but he shall eat the flesh of the fat, and tear their claws in pieces.*

39. MALACHI
God wants you to be whole. He wants to bless you in all your pertinent parts, spiritually, mentally, and physically. There is healing for every area of your life.

Malachi 4:2, *But unto you that fear my name shall the sun of righteousness arise with healing in his wings; and ye shall go forth, and grow up as calves of the stall.*

New Testament

Divine Healing continues to flow like a sparkling river throughout the New Testament.

40. MATTHEW
We are the hands and feet of Jesus on this earth. We should walk throughout this earth laying our hands upon people who are sick and believing God for their healing. Jesus Christ is the same yesterday, today and forever.

Matthew 8;13, *And Jesus said unto the centurion, Go thy way; and as thou hast believed, so be it done unto thee. And his servant was healed in the selfsame hour.*

Matthew 9:35, *And Jesus went about all the cities and villages, teaching in their synagogues, and preaching the gospel of the kingdom, and healing every sickness and every disease among the people.*

41. MARK
Mark 16:15-18 is called the Great Commission. We are Christ's ambassadors who have been given authority to use His name to cast out devils and heal the sick.

Mark 16:17-18, *And these signs shall follow them that believe; In my name shall they cast out devils; they shall speak with new tongues;*
v. 18, *They shall take up serpents; and if they drink any deadly thing, it shall not hurt them; they shall lay hands on the sick, and they shall recover.*

42. LUKE
Luke was a physician, and the book of Luke is full of testimonies about the healing power of Jesus. He said that Jesus healed all who touched Him.

Luke 6:19, *And the whole multitude sought to touch him: for there went virtue out of him, and healed them all.*

43. JOHN

You will have abundant life when Jesus heals your spirit, soul, and body. Abundant life is abundant living.

John 10:10, *The thief cometh not, but for to kill, and to destroy: I am come that they might have life, and that they might have it more abundantly.*

44. ACTS

Salvation and healing go together. When you have mighty healings, then you are going to have mighty salvations, because the healings will cause men to believe and trust in God. The book of Acts is full of great healings.

Acts 3:6, *Then Peter said, Silver and gold have I none; but such as I have give I thee: In the name of Jesus Christ of Nazareth rise up and walk.*

45. ROMANS

The perfect will of God is that man should be as God made him to be; well and happy and aggressive to live for Him. Be full of faith and don't let anyone put unbelief in your heart.

Romans 12:1-2, *I beseech you therefore, brethren, by the mercies of God, that ye present your bodies a living sacrifice, holy, acceptable unto God, which is your reasonable service.*

v. 2, *And be not conformed to this world: but be ye transformed by the renewing of your mind, that ye may prove what is that good, and acceptable, and perfect, will of God.*

46. I CORINTHIANS

The gifts of healing were given to the Church of Jesus Christ to bless the people of God. God wants us to be whole and not full of disease. Provision has been made for your spirit, soul, and body to be healthy before the Lord.

I Corinthians 12:8-10, *For to one is given by the Spirit the word of wisdom; to another the word of knowledge by the same Spirit;*

v. 9, *To another faith by the same Spirit; to another the gifts of healing by the same Spirit;*

v. 10, *To another the working of miracles; to another prophecy; to another discerning of spirits; to another divers kinds of tongues; to another the interpretation of tongues.*

47. II CORINTHIANS

The Lord Jesus owned all of heaven and

He came down here, not to impoverish you, but to prosper you and to make you rich. One of the best ways to be prosperous is to be healthy.

II Corinthians 8:9-15, *For ye know the grace of our Lord Jesus Christ, that, though he was rich yet for your sakes he became poor, that ye through his poverty might be rich.*

v. 10, *And herein I give my advice: for this is expedient for you, who have begun before, not only to do, but also to be forward a year ago.*

v. 11, *Now therefore perform the doing of it; that as there was a readiness to will, so there may be a performance also out of that which ye have.*

v. 12, *For if there be first a willing mind, it is accepted according to that a man hath, and not according to that he hath not.*

v. 13, *For I mean not that other men be eased, and ye burdened:*

v. 14, *But by an equality, that now at this time your abundance may be a supply for their want, that their abundance also may be a supply for your want: that there may be equality:*

v. 15, *As it is written, He that had gathered much had nothing over; and he that had gathered little had no lack.*

48. GALATIANS

If God has provided healing for you by the stripes of Jesus, then you are already healed. The Word says you are healed and Paul claims that anyone preaching any other Gospel, even if it would be an angel, he is accursed. So if you are an unbeliever, do not spread your unbelief.

Galatians 1:8, *But though we, or an angel from heaven, preach any other gospel unto you than that which we have preached unto you, let him be accursed.*

49. EPHESIANS

Our battle is not a natural warfare, but a spiritual one. Satan seeks to destroy our health, our happiness, and everything that we have. In the name of Jesus, we command ourselves to be healed and to stay well by His mighty power.

Ephesians 5:12, *For we wrestle not against flesh and blood, but against principalities, against powers, against the rulers of the darkness of this world, against spiritual wickedness in high places.*

50. PHILIPPIANS

When Jesus was resurrected from the dead, He came forth from the grave with the keys to death and hell. He also has the keys to the Kingdom of God. All power in heaven and earth and under the earth belongs to Him. Seek to know Him, and the power of His resurrection!

Philippians 3:10, *That I may know him, and the power of his resurrection, and the fellowship of his sufferings, being made conformable unto his death;*

51. COLOSSIANS

All things were created by God, and by Him all things consist. That means your health, your healing, your joy, and your well-being. The Lord Jesus Christ is King of kings and Lord of lords, the Healer of healers. He is the one who supplies the life and strength that you and I enjoy today.

Colossians 1:3-4, *We give thanks to God and the father of our Lord Jesus Christ praying always for you,*
v. 4, *Since we heard of your faith in Christ Jesus, and of the love which ye have to all the saints . . .*

Colossians 1:16-17, *For by him were all things created, that are in heaven, and that are in earth, visible and invisible, whether they be thrones, or dominions, or principalities, or powers: all things were created by him, and for him:*
v. 17, *And he is before all things, and by him all things consist.*

52. I THESSALONIANS

Imagine having a spirit, soul, and body that is blameless. Blameless means to have perfect health. Paul prayed that the Thessalonians would be preserved totally whole, through sanctification, until Jesus comes.

I Thessalonians 5:23, *And the very God of peace sanctify you wholly; and I pray God your whole spirit and soul and body be preserved blameless unto the coming of our Lord Jesus Christ.*

53. II THESSALONIANS

God wants to be glorified in us. There is not much glory in broken limbs and diseases that destroy the body. I have lived in over one hundred nations of the world, and many times our living conditions were very primitive and the food was poor, but I have enjoyed fifty years of health. That's glorifying God!

II Thessalonians 1:12, *That the name of our Lord Jesus Christ may be glorified in you, and ye in him, according to the grace of our God and the Lord Jesus Christ.*

54. I TIMOTHY

Paul told Timothy to hold his faith. You are healed by faith and kept well by faith. Paul said that some people had abandoned their faith and were shipwrecked. Be sure your faith is strong in the Lord and in the power of His might.

I Timothy 1:19, *Holding faith, and a good conscience; which some having put away concerning faith have made ship-wreck . . .*

55. II TIMOTHY

Fear does not come from God, but He has given us three things: the spirit of power (that's authority), the spirit of love (that's the nature of God), and the spirit of a sound mind (we can think straight).

II Timothy 1:7, *For God hath not given us the spirit of fear; but of power, and of love, and of a sound mind.*

56. TITUS

If you want to stay well, deny ungodliness and worldly lust and live soberly. Living soberly does not just mean to avoid alcoholic beverages, but also to live a righteous and godly life. Don't live for this life alone, but remember that you are but a stranger here. You are going to a better land, which is heaven. That will make you happy and keep the blessing of God flowing through you.

Titus 2:11-13, *For the grace of God that bringeth salvation hath appeared to all men,*

v. 12, *Teaching us that, denying ungod-liness and worldly lusts, we should live so-berly, righteously, and godly, in this present world;*

v. 13, *Looking for that blessed hope, and the glorious appearing of the great God and our Saviour Jesus Christ.*

57. PHILEMON

Having a loving attitude toward the Lord and all of God's people will keep you healthy. If you are at peace with your world, your entire being will function better.

Philemon 5-6, *Hearing of thy love and faith, which thou hast toward the Lord Jesus, and toward all saints;*

v. 6, *That the communication of thy faith may become effectual by the acknow-ledging of every good thing which is in you in Christ Jesus.*

58. HEBREWS

Jesus Christ has not changed. Whatever He did in Galilee, Judea, or Jerusalem, He will do in your town because He is the same yesterday, today, and forever. If Jesus healed sick people in Jerusalem, He is obligated to heal you when you call upon His name. There is healing in the name of Jesus.

Hebrews 13:8, *Jesus Christ the same yesterday, and to day, and for ever.*

59. JAMES

James is very specific in saying that when you are sick, pray about it. Don't sit around worrying or feeling sad, but pray. He also tells us to call for the leaders of the church. They are to pray and anoint the sick with oil in the name of the Lord. The anointing oil is applied as a symbol of the Holy Spirit, believing that the power and the authority and the strength of the Holy Spirit will flow into you until you are healed.

James 5:13-15, *Is any among you afflicted? let him pray. Is any merry? let him sing psalms.*

v. 14, *Is any sick among you? let him call for the elders of the church; and let them pray over him, anointing him with oil in the name of the Lord:*

v. 15, *And the prayer of faith shall save the sick, and the Lord shall raise him up; and if he have committed sins, they shall be forgiven him.*

60. I PETER

I Peter 2:24 is one of the golden texts of healing in the Bible. Since God is love and God has power, it only seems natural that we should believe that God is a mighty deliverer and a great healer.

I Peter 2:24, *Who his own self bare our sins in his own body on the tree, that we, being dead to sins, should live unto righteousness: by whose stripes ye were healed.*

61. II PETER

The Lord wants us to know that He is not slack concerning any promise He has made in the entire Bible. You have a promise of healing and it's yours. I hope you will cling to His promises and let them bless you.

II Peter 3:9, *The Lord is not slack concerning his promise, as some men count slackness; but is longsuffering to us-ward, not willing that any should perish, but that all should come to repentance.*

62. I JOHN

The reason God sent Jesus Christ to earth was for Him to destroy the works of the devil. He came to set men free from bondage, whether it be spiritual, mental, or physical. Be free in Jesus' name!

I John 3:8, *He that committeth sin is of the devil; for the devil sinneth from the beginning. For this purpose the Son of God was manifested, that he might destroy the works of the devil.*

63. II JOHN

Don't go through life being partially blessed. Receive a full reward, a full measure! God wants you to have everything He has prepared for you.

II John 8, *Look to yourselves, that we lose not those things we have wrought, but that we receive a full reward.*

64. III JOHN

John points out that to stay healthy, our soul must prosper. The soul consists of the mind, emotions, and will. Isaiah 26:3 promises that when our mind is stayed on the Lord and we trust in Him, we shall have perfect peace. Our soul needs to be ruled by our spirit, which in turn must be controlled by the Holy Spirit. As the God of peace rules our lives, we will experience health and prosperity.

III John 2, *Beloved, I wish above all things that thou mayest prosper and be in health, even as thy soul prospereth.*

65. JUDE

As we have faith in God, and earnestly contend for the faith, we are candidates to receive the promises related to faith.

Jude 3, 20, *Beloved, when I gave all diligence to write unto you of the common sal-*

vation, it was needful for me to write unto you, and exhort you that ye should earnestly contend for the faith which was once delivered unto the saints.

v. 20, *But ye, beloved, building up yourselves on your most holy faith, praying in the Holy Ghost.*

66. REVELATION

When Christ comes from heaven to receive us unto Himself, He wants to find His people without spot or wrinkle. He is coming for a people rejoicing in victory and power. The Lord is looking for faithful soldiers who can say, *I have fought a good fight, I have finished my course, I have kept the faith: Henceforth there is laid up for me a crown of righteousness . . .* (II Tim. 4:7-8). Through Christ Jesus, we have the victory!

Revelation 22:12, *And, behold, I come quickly; and my reward is with me, to give every man according as his work shall be.*

Dr. Lester Sumrall
1913-1996

Stephen Sumrall

The
Vision
Continues...

*He will be very gracious to you at the sound of
your cry; When He hears it, He will answer you.*
— Isaiah 30:19 NKJV

What a glorious promise from our gracious
God! He will hear our cries, and He *will*
answer. When I consider the overwhelming
numbers of requests for help that cross my
desk here at Feed The Hungry, I am com-
forted to know that it is not this organization
that is responding to the cries of the world's
hungry; God is responding through us. When
we follow His will, miracles happen.

Since the creation of Feed The Hungry in 1987, we have witnessed countless examples of God's people being used to feed starving families around the world. In Abakan, Siberia, families were in desperate need of food and warm winter clothing. We responded by sending thousands of pounds of supplies — including canned goods, rice, wheat, new winter clothing, vitamins, and Russian-language Bibles. For many, that shipment was a gift of life during the harsh Siberian winter.

We were able to undertake a massive outreach to the starving families of Liberia, Africa, where they had experienced years of civil war. Four million pounds of relief was shipped aboard LeSEA's missionary vessel *Evangeline*, and the sight of the great ship in the harbor caused our hearts to swell with gratitude to the Almighty for the multitude of faithful people who made the project a success.

FTH has delivered food and encouragement to helpless victims of devastating and deadly earthquakes, floods, drought, hurricanes, and to hopeless refugees of conflict and persecution. We celebrate the privilege of having been God's instrument of salvation for thousands of souls who have opened their hearts to receive the Bread of life.

God has opened doors and made a way for us to minister to kings, to impact the course of nations, and to carry the gospel to the far corners of the globe. We have trusted in God's protection as we traveled into uncertain and even dangerous situations, and have felt His presence and approval.

Several pastors from churches in Oaxaca, Mexico wrote to me expressing their gratitude for a shipment of food we sent to them. They said, "Many families in our churches are suffering from hunger. Our country is in economic crisis and our state of Oaxaca is one of the poorest states of our nation. God has heard the cry of our people in moving upon your hearts to extend this hand of blessing to us."

This letter, like all the letters of appreciation we receive, is for you. Your gifts and prayers are helping extend a hand of blessing . . . as "God hears the cry of His people." But even as we celebrate each child who is fed, each pastor who can help his flock, and every family who will have its daily bread, we do not rest. The prayers of the poor and suffering continue to move our hearts.

Please know that any gift you can send today will be the answer to someone's prayers.

Thank you, and may God bless you for reaching out with Christ's compassion to those in need.

Always for the hungry,

Stephen Sumrall
President,
LeSEA Global Feed The Hungry®

LESEA GLOBAL
FEED _{THE} HUNGRY®

1-888-TEAM-FTH
1-888-8326-384
www.feedthehungry.org

Dr. Lester Sumrall (1913-1996) traveled the world as a missionary statesman for over sixty years and saw firsthand the terrible suffering caused by hunger and poverty. In 1987, he was challenged by God with a vision to feed those innocent people who are plagued by such desperate situations. With enthusiasm and determination, Lester Sumrall founded LeSea Global Feed The Hungry® that same year.

In the intervening years, the ministry has re-sponded to needs in over 70 nations around the world. Dr. Sumrall's vision has delivered over 140 million dollars of relief supplies.

LeSea Global Feed The Hungry, a division of LeSea, Inc., is a non-profit 501(c)(3), Christian mission organization.
We directly oversee the entire relief process, making sure contributions get into the hands of those in need without political intervention. Before a distribution takes place, we secure guarantees from the appropriate government agencies, giving us the rights to distribute the food directly to the local pastors. Having volunteer directors in more than thirty countries allows us to respond almost immediately to disaster situations around the world.

Other books by Dr. Lester Sumrall –

Adventuring With Christ
Be Bold and Walk Tall
Courage to Conquer
Demons: The Answer Book
Faith Can Change Your World
The Gifts and Ministries of the Holy Spirit
God's Blueprint for a Happy Home
The Life Story of Lester Sumrall
The Militant Church
Mystery of Death
Pioneers of Faith
Angels to Help You
Run With the Vision
Spirit, Soul, and Body
Unprovoked Murder
You Can Destroy the Gates of Hell
60 Things God Said about Sex
101 Questions & Answers on Demon Power
Secrets of Answered Prayer

To receive a catalog of available materials,
contact:

Sumrall Publishing
P.O. Box 12, South Bend, IN 46624
www.sumrallpublishing.com